The Port Side of Shadows

Poems of Travel—

Inner, Outer and Uncharted Places

poems by

Patricia Williams

Finishing Line Press
Georgetown, Kentucky

The Port Side of Shadows

Poems of Travel—

Inner, Outer and Uncharted Places

Copyright © 2017 by Patricia Williams
ISBN 978-1-63534-164-5 First Edition
All rights reserved under International and Pan-American Copyright Conventions.
No part of this book may be reproduced in any manner whatsoever without written permission from the publisher, except in the case of brief quotations embodied in critical articles and reviews.

ACKNOWLEDGMENTS

My thanks to the editors of the following publications in which these poems first appeared, at times in a slightly altered version:

Avocet Weekly: "Home Sweet Home"
Journeys Along the Silk Road: "Sketches Along the Yangtze"
Mused: "Lyon Gastronomique"
Red Booth Review: "Some Things Die Before Called"
Silver Blade: "Lorca's Duende"
Wisconsin Fellowship of Poets 2016 Calendar: "Missing Home"

Publisher: Leah Maines

Editor: Christen Kincaid

Cover Art: Patricia Williams

Author Photo: Patricia Williams

Cover Design: Patricia Williams

Printed in the USA on acid-free paper.
Order online: www.finishinglinepress.com
　　　　also available on amazon.com

　　　　　　　　Author inquiries and mail orders:
　　　　　　　　　　Finishing Line Press
　　　　　　　　　　　P. O. Box 1626
　　　　　　　　　Georgetown, Kentucky 40324
　　　　　　　　　　　　U. S. A.

Table of Contents

Expatriate 1
Magic in Collapsing Stars 2
Night Music 3
Some Things Die Before Called 4
A Green Chiffon Dress 5
Perils and Choices 6
Out of Reach 7
Challenging Dragons 8
In Dreams There Dwells a Magic Force 9
Twelve O'clock Travel 10
Melville's Destination 11
Wayfarers 12
Essaouira 13
Alfred's World 14
Visit to Cordoba: Faded Light 15
Dancing Flamenco in Ronda 16
Lorca's *Duende* 17
Impermanence 18
Midlife Crisis 19
The Oracle Answers 20
Watching *The Misanthrope* in French 21
Lyon *Gastronomique* 22
The Saints Said Nothing 23
Home Sweet Home 24
Classic Cinematic Love Affair 25
Renewal 26
Sketches along the Yangtze 27

*To the friends and colleagues
who have helped me find my way
along a new path—*

Expatriate
> "Serenely let us move to distant places and let
> no sentiments of home detain us…prepare
> for parting and leave-taking or else
> remain the slave of permanence" —Hermann Hess

Rows of brick bungalows and two-flats,
an occasional white cottage, the corner store,
all in city-block order—

narrow back-alleys and
streets lined with spring-flowered catalpa trees,
their blossom clusters, like cymbidium orchids,
their leaves, heart-shaped—

mothers in tidy houses sweep front walkways,
yet falling red mulberries
still stain children's shoes—

what we have left, those who have left us,
images of long-past selves—
we carry them all, scattered through life
like last year's snow.

Magic in Collapsing Stars

> *"Somewhere, something incredible is waiting to be known."* —Carl Sagan

We are made of the stuff of stars,
a taste of the wild, covered in forests
and meadows where violets sigh.

We are solitary nights, silent,
the quiet of space broken only by
the hoot of an owl.

We occupy a minute place,
not lofty, not specially charmed.
Stay—be here with me
                —just breathing.

Night Music

Nightfall is the finest time to visit our country haven.
We escape to forest green that shrouds the eaves—
leave the clatter of a settled world.

I dream of unwinding there, nestled deep in a downy settee,
hearing a symphony of darkness—
web-footed songsters and untamed canines sing cantatas
under an effervescent sky.

We sip blush wine in the nippy breath of night
by light from a fire's flicker
and watch shadows slant across our reverie.

Some Things Die Before Called

Big box stores
ran end-of-winter sales,
the groundhog predicted
spring was soon to come,
the calendar revealed
winter's conclusion—

but winter never ended,
spring never came.

April drizzle,
not sweet and languid,
but sleety and raw
like February,
spat ice and snow—

winter never ended,
spring never came.

The globe is murky,
the solar star frozen,
the lunar orb immobilized.
We long for something
not to be found—

you left in winter;
spring never came.

A Green Chiffon Dress

Opera is broadcast live
on Public Radio.
When I tune in, I recall grand,
long-past evenings.

Fans, dressed to the nines
—some in long gowns, some in tuxedos—
clapped, shouted "bravo",
sipped champagne during intermission.

I remember an elegant outfit I wore
on one occasion,
an emerald-green dress
—chiffon and taffeta, simply-cut,
just past the knee—
green satin shoes
—high-heeled, pointy-toed—
green and blue crystal necklace,
flashing.

Opera's part of a past life.
When I hear certain arias, certain duets,
tears well
—not for the melody's sweetness—
for the sweetness of the life
I left behind.

Perils and Choices

We took our last ride of childhood
                on a merry-go-round
                      in the park
    —emerged along tortuous roads,
        down a darkened, wet street,
    cobble-stoned—
                vanished into a world
of wrong turns and small talk
              —of butterflies who flutter for a day—
            where
the ring of footfalls retreating in the dark,
    evaporates
             in an empty moonlit square
                we might mistake
            for distant snow.

Out of Reach

Shadows play in painted light
        that filters through the trees
            at sundown—
bathes every living thing
in the molten gold of a sunflower field
      —fades—
        gives way to hovering darkness.

The mirrored moon floats on water,
       —visible but untouchable—
            washed in the piercing pain
       of wanting something
            you can't have.

Challenging Dragons

I search for a blue blossom
unsullied by purple tints,
a city night untainted by reflection,
dark enough to see the stars.

I look for you in a dozen faces—
sometimes see a glimmer,
that on closer inspection,
evaporates like a snowflake
when we try to catch it.

Exhausted by pain and discontent,
I let go—
not a flower unfolding,
a dragon, clawing.

In Dreams There Dwells a Magic Force

        She wandered, barefoot,
        dampening the sound of footsteps
        in night's angles—

stood with studied carelessness
in a place of sulky darkness
roaming in search of mystery—
wistful, adrift.

        "I am a dry leaf," she said,
        "rustled by a shallow breath,
        extinguishing torches,
        mystifying enemies—

              travel agent for the dead,
              I whisper the language of dreams,
              homesick for a place I've never been."

Twelve O'clock Travel

In the half-light of forbidden places,
I explore murky corners,
unearth hidden turnings, sail on the edge of slumber,
drowse languid in time.

A presence sounds in a stone-spiked grotto,
prowls this reverie.
Twists and bends plunge me deep in cavernous scenery,
an icy river trickles through a ravine.

Alone in my midnight wanderings, anxious to escape,
I ask the resonant emptiness,
"Where is higher ground,
where is the way to the cleansing sea?"

Melville's Destination

Beyond the wilds of Summerland,
in a twelve o 'clock sky
    dusky as a raven's wing,
        lies a singular place where time dissolves,
            tears, in a drop of rain—

where scraps of wisdom inscribed on parchment
note the struggles of a fallen snowbird.

Sound and fragrance
drench the air with unbearable sweetness,
    glide on forbidden seas,
    alight on barbarous shores,
        mark a trail of broken blossoms—

there, moonflower-like, we fade after a single evening.
    "Not on any map, as true places never are." *

*Herman Melville

Wayfarers

Three dozen doves rise in unison,
    a gray-feathered canopy
        winging toward a struggling sun,
            as red dusk fills the sky.
Flightless, we wander
    adrift in an earth-bound limbo,
        searching for direction,
    —nomads roaming boulevards—

the act of travelling
    more important
        than the destination.

Essaouira*

I receive impulses from the world—
    eavesdrop on
        the workings of this existence,
  explore the port side of shadows—
      along my way to Essaouira.

The velvet dark embraces trepidation,
    foreboding I cannot explain—
        silent witness to changing seasons
  —a reflection of the unknown.

I hear trees grow—
    they twist and bend across the gritty distance,
        wait in this place of imagination,
  this place of ultraviolet light—and I pause.

I chase ghosts through the night,
    tread softly, listen closely as I walk—
        remember gulls that swoop the beach,
  white goats in argan trees,
        in this place that's called Essaouira.

*Essaouira is a Moroccan city, pronounced *ess-we-rah*

Alfred's World
> *A common sight across the moors—disturbing when the wings move to town**

I saw starlings gather at Coventry in the West Midlands of England.
Ebony feathers navigated moorlands, iridescent motion
generated shapes in synchronized activity.

Moving as one in pulsating antics, they formed hourglass and funnel
and ribbon designs, midair—an avian dance, dizzy in the evening sky,
a murmuring bird ballet.

A thousand wings moved to city tree tops, some withdrew, more
arrived on the scene—autumn-bared boughs drooped, weighed down
with black feather foliage.

Unsettled, I shifted to shelter, turned locks, covered windows,
hid from the cinematic sight as an encore formed in the distance.

I saw starlings gather at Coventry in the West Midlands of England—
no one knows why they murmur.

---

*Starling flocks in tight, fluid formations are called *murmurations*.

Visit to Cordoba: Faded Light

Tenants of crowded cities
crave desolate places, solitary nights,
conjure sensual visions
of starry, desert skies.

Desert-dwellers,
captives in their world of darkness,
long for the gardens of Cordoba,
for red and white arches
under soft Moorish light.

I searched for a beacon,
for Al-Andalus, that sliver of luminosity,
pathway between worlds,
that whisper of edified thought—
faded,
       vanished,
              vaporized.

Dancing Flamenco in Ronda

        I went to Andalusia to breathe the spirit,
to feel the aura of Spanish hill towns.

In Ronda, a sky island perched on sheer cliffs,
        spanning a canyon,
                I found flamenco in a smoky *taverna*—

        the singer's scorched voice,
the passion of a guitar
                thick with soul-wrenching sorrow,
a dancer whose prime had passed—

        unaware of anything around her, she
              danced the rhythm of her beating heart,

        danced as if life depended on dancing—
              as if death might come any moment.

Lorca's *Duende*

An eerie and baffling sadness
       —a sadness that dwells in the spirit,
            a hold that grips the throat,
     emptiness that follows tears,
leaves lifeblood frozen.

The soul's suffering
      —its acute awareness of death—
in a heightened state of emotion,
     in a heightened state of expression,
         holds both agony and splendor.

All that has dark sound
     echoes through shadowed alleys,
         accepts limitations of reason—
   a sorrow that brings raw pain
rouses throbbing anguish.

          Some will know its soulfulness,
     only when they are old, as I am—
the twisting knife of reality,
       the frayed sound of nightfall.

Impermanence

I've watched them soar at home
and in far-off places.
      They tilt side to side as they float,

          trace lazy rounds on the skin of the sky,
          silent sailboats, six feet across.

     I saw them once from the top of a temple
circling charnel grounds in Tibet—
not messengers of bereavement,
      but a sacred crew that attends the dead—

          dressed in mourning,
          they glide elegant on warm drafts.

     I see them silently soaring,
and think of sky burials—
spirits riding on columns of air.

Midlife Crisis

Everyone has a *mezzo cammin,*
the halfway mark in life—
      a time no one can define,
no one can predict,
          occurs anywhere after
     raw innocence.

     Treading water,
fluttering with cautious delight,
the heart whispers—
          there is a song,
a leaping thought, a novel possibility.

The mind shouts, protests
—a polished steel curve—
      dreams dangle out of reach,
        teasing,
fade away into dusty curtains.

The Oracle Answers

Heaven and Earth touch at Delphi,
        a towering place of ancient ruins
where valleys of olive and cypress
            meet the wine-dark sea,
    where humans
        once felt the gods breathing,
    heard honey-voiced singing
        and Pythia's whispered answers—

"Insight is above pearls and gold,
        somewhere between confident expectation
            and wishful thinking—
    It is night and day,
        dusk and dawn
grounded in the ordinary, in the familiar,
        in the mundane that never is—"

    Some believe spirits still live at Delphi—
that ancient magic murmurs
    when charmed vapors rise—
            when pale oleander
    scents the motion-filled air.

Watching *The Misanthrope* in French

Molière's statue greets theatregoers
    at the *Comedie Francaise* in Paris—

seeing the scarlet carpet,
    painted ceiling,
        the ornate chandelier—
is worth the price of a ticket.

    The play was Moliere's *Misanthrope*,
        performed in classical verse,
and there I sat,
    with two years of high school French
        studied twenty-five years before.

I strained to catch a phrase here and there
    —understood
        about every tenth word—
    then relaxed,
forgot about translation,

        used my ears to enjoy pure sound,
    let my eyes drink in the action—

physical encounter, easy to grasp in any language.

Lyon *Gastronomique*

> "How do you govern a country that has
> two-hundred and forty-six varieties of cheese?"
> —Charles de Gaulle

I remember my days in Lyon—
classical ruins on the sheer hillside,
Renaissance routes from street to street,
kaleidoscope colors of the ancient silk trade,
    —and most of all—
farmer's markets filled with splendor.

Premium beef, poultry of Bresse,
twenty-two species of potato,
deep-lake fish from the French Alps district,
wine from vineyards terraced in Roman times,
    —and cheese, beautiful cheese—
in shades from cream to amber.

Camembert and brie, munster and chèvre,
blue-veined cheeses of the central region,
cheese produced by one lone farmer
from a single herd of cows
    —all with names—
that roam freely in the mountains.

The Saints Said Nothing

Thirty sacred statues
—weathered stone and dusky metal—
border the Charles Bridge
along the path to Prague Castle.
Travelers throng the crossway
under the gaze of soundless saints.

Churches and chapels abound
in wood-carved sanctity and relic bones.
The Holy Infant in brocaded silk,
jewel-laden Madonnas,
avenging archangels in armor,
look down from ornate altars
—painted mouths, frescoed faces—
keep tomb-like silence.
Wenceslas the good king,
saintly equestrian, shield of the lowly,
quietly presides over New Town Square.

The apostle clock in Old Town
continues its medieval routine.
Twelve robotic disciples
parade in mechanical order,
raise automated hands
to bless crowds gathered below
as Death strikes the hour,

as empty eyes of clerics and lawmakers
watched trains depart for Terezin. *

*Czech name for Theresienstadt concentration camp located northwest of Prague; served as a waystation to the death camps of Auschwitz and Treblinka. Few of the 15,000 children sent to Terezin survived

Home Sweet Home Concerto in Three Movements and Coda

I
Forest interiors
shelter tree trunks split by lightning,
strangely shaped lifeless wood.
Lichen patches, like dermal abrasions,
creep and encrust ancient grayed timber.
Deadly mushrooms in lurid hues,
threaten the unaware.

II
If you've never seen red sumac leaves
fierce with autumn,
then you've never seen vermillion.
Take a swig of the color,
sniff the scene, eye, don't finger—
lush crimson colonies
brocaded with jade and gold,
scaling tree shafts, disguising ditch slopes,
might just be venomous ivy.

III
Gnarled pines widen at root level—
sun drops down, rocks abandon the day's heat,
wind whirls overhead.
Frosted landscapes, fractured
like shattered glass, conjure a scrapbook
of the season's bullying chill—
snow brings a four-coat winter.

Coda
A place of harsh beauty like no other.

Classic Cinematic Love Affair

                    We'll meet again,
even if we live life mostly in our heads,
do nothing more adventurous
            than feed small birds—
    maybe when
Harry Lime steps from a doorway in Vienna
            —revealed
    by a feline's loving rub—

          we'll meet again,
    don't know where, don't know when
        —two shadows on a Ferris wheel—
    as time goes by
in some other place,
    on some other stage
—swift-moving black sails on the horizon,
    flying an ominous banner,
                we'll head for Rick's Café—
                      breathing—
breathing slowly
    and deeply and smoothly.

Renewal

Their inhospitable form made Chinese mountains
sacred sites—nearness to paradise ordained them
home to immortals.

Tai Shan, crest of heaven, facing the rising sun—
    place of origin and renewal,
        untold temples embrace the slopes.

Pilgrims climbed seven-thousand steps—
    marked with poems and prayers
        carved large and golden in living rock—
    before Greeks hallowed Olympus,
        before Fujiyama was sanctified.

Incense burns to the Jade Goddess,
    sheltered in a temple on the mountain brow—
        supplicants bind branches
with scarlet prayer ribbons,
    settle into ledges during darkness,
sleep 'til daybreak, wake to watch the sun
    rise from the sea.

Pilgrims gasp for beauty, hearts pierced,
as the solar disk slices through dawn-kissed, lilac clouds,
marvel at the unblemished morning light—
        return refreshed to the ashen world below.

Sketches along the Yangtze

I. Solitude

Nothing but the moon attends
ten thousand peaks along the river.
Forlorn wanderers in the gorges
weep for home
when the gibbon's cry echoes.
Only in this place can a traveler
hear sound so mournful.

II. Myth

The gorges run deep and long,
sunlight rarely penetrates
—the pinnacles,
green-clad and shrouded
in a curtain of rain.

Here, an Immortal loved a mortal king
and invaded his dreams
as a cloud at dawn and rain at sunset.
Clouds and rain have since begotten
a symphony of longing.

III. Renewal

Ahead are the twelve peaks of Wu Gorge,
a bleak and frothy, dark place.
The aura heavy, somber, desolate—
waves churn, roar, and rush to the sky.

Over the frontier pass,
wind and clouds sink to the waiting earth
where traces of million-year ancestries
embrace ancient terrain.
The mighty Yangtze crashes,
carves its way to the sea.

Patricia Williams, originally from Illinois, was, for 27 years, a professor of Design at the University of Wisconsin—Stevens Point. Although always a vociferous reader, she did not begin writing poetry until early in 2013, after she retired from teaching.

"I feel that art, design, music and the literary arts are natural partners—all creatively examine life and living. Poetry is a search for the universal in the personal. Some poems can be taken at face value, some have layers. Each of us reads a poem through our own life filter and each takes away a different understanding or experience."

Williams' poems have been published in a variety of print and online journals and anthologies. *The Port Side of Shadows*, her first chapbook, reflects traveling not only in the physical sense, but in those "uncharted places" of the spirit and the imagination.

She lives with her husband in rural central Wisconsin, where she is at work on a new chapbook about country living. Williams has three sons, daughters-in-law and grandchildren.

www.ingramcontent.com/pod-product-compliance
Lightning Source LLC
LaVergne TN
LVHW041514070426
835507LV00012B/1554